Kade
Berman

REASON
& PASSION

 A catalogue record for this book is available from the National Library of Australia

Berman, Kade (author)
Reason & Passion
ISBN 978-0-6451513-7-4
Poetry

Typeset Addington 10/14

Edited by Matthew Bassat
Cover and book design by Green Hill Publishing

Illustrations:
on pages 3, 11, 15, 19, 27, 39, 59, 85, 93, 105, 109, 113, 117, 121 - by Ella Hermann
on pages 7, 31, 35, 47, 63, 67, 71, 79, 101 - by Hannah Bourbon
on pages 51, 75, 129 - by Nadine Alford
on pages 23, 89, 97 - by Kade Berman
on pages 43, 125 - by Mia Komesaroff
on pages 55 - by Malli Rubinstein

Contents

The Entombment of the Forest 5

Nature 9

Gratitude 13

Spring 17

Cycles 21

A Wave of Love 25

Goals 29

Purpose 33

Time 37

Reason and Passion 41

Wilting Leaves 45

Love's Nuance 49

Belief 53

Defenceless Joy 57

Burning Cloth 61

Oh, Father 65

Icarus 69

Shame 73

Tenuous Love 77

Death 81

The Broken Scale 87

Kindness 91

Unknowns 95

Words 99

Giving 103

Leadership 107

Waves 111

New Life 115

Family 119

Wonders of a Sunset 123

Distant Love 127

Candles 131

Kade Berman is an author from Melbourne, Australia. He started writing his first book *Reason and Passion* whilst on a year away, volunteering in developing countries. That experience helped inspire his outlook of peoplehood, the beauty of nature and the realness of the world. Kade is passionate about harnessing the power of language to propel others into action, whether that be through personal development or social advocacy.

REASON & PASSION

The Entombment of the Forest

Its primordial beauty encourages quiet reflection
yet its precarious equilibrium wants for loudest
protection.

The delicate strokes of the leaves reflect a green
lustrous spark
still, the looming conflagration casts a grim shadow of
blackened bark.

Grass elevating to a natural fort
is cut by the egregious razor that shreds the grass to a
voiceless retort.

The wonderful branches that tremble and bloom
are replaced by the mangled roots that machines
exhume.

Prettily, how the purple coats the flowery iridescent
bed
yet it suddenly bleeds; a mosaic of ceaseless choking
red.

And whilst the forest yet spans a vast range,
its heart is overturned to a metropolitan milieu; a
sordid exchange.

To protect, we must first admire the complexity of the
    green Earth,
that hides within the tapestry of the forest and waits to
    present its worth.

However, in our blindness we have voyaged to an
    interminable blight;
bereft of the green backdrop, we are bound for a
    solemn, unalterable night.

Nature

Nature projects a glow of incumbent awe
from the patterned Sapa terraces to the Halong river
    floor.

Her delicate stroke so gentle yet strong
animates water, ground and sky, where the sentient
    belong.

To distinguish the simplest green from green and blue
    from blue,
the flourish spreads; leaf, stem and seed are born anew.

The whistling trees and the steadily crashing waves
    have much to say;
the auburn-shadowed rocks and supple lilies afloat
    have as much to convey.

The tremulous autumnal leaves sift down to the ocean
    floor
whilst the rivers' tidal breath scatters light stones on
    river shores.

As the peaceful white swans ripple the shoals with
    easy tread,
above are the melodious dancing birds, dotting the
    skies in a liberated stead.

Sitting on a weed-bedded rock, absorbing all there is
    to see,
a man enjoys the splendour of nature's toils; it is where
    he ought to be.

Gratitude

Tired of youth and its encumbering, unending
    duration,
a young boy prayed with artless determination:

that he would speedily traverse the inevitable passage
    of time
and grow old in a moment's effortless climb.

But when his callow wish was granted,
by a piercing regret was his vain hope supplanted.

Magically, his body transformed into a pernicious
    elderly cage;
an impatient wish to grow up had brought him to
    death's wintry stage.

To have avoided such a curse, there had been but one
    way:
to have relished his youth, to have prized each day.

The other children gathered around in silent dismay
to see their friend whose once-lively spirit was now
    permanently at bay.

Undaunted, the old man sat impassively by a sugar
    maple tree
whilst his friends encircled him, resting pensively on
    eager knees.

"Listen to me," he exhorted, "for it is nearly my time to
    go:
you must be grateful for who you are and cherish the
    life you know."

As the mystified children sat, luxuriating in the tree's
    cool shade,
they listened intently to the wise words, at once
    enthralled and afraid.

"How lucky you are to be so young, and lit with youth's
    soulful flame;
do not wish it over and see it snuffed out: an ambition
    that many a life would maim."

So the old man, now contented, could readily part with
    fears subdued;
his friends would live a long and wonderful life,
    equipped with the virtue of gratitude.

Spring

A soft blue with a whip of violet hinging on the
    horizon floor,
and a profusion of weightless, mighty clouds sailing
    over the painted atmospheric decor.

The sun's scintillation reflects onto the rolling hills and
    shines to double the flowing river,
where the excited children run and the lone toads
    shiver.

The intermission between the bright summer shine
    and the silent winter bite
is spring, a quarter that emulates wonders; a harp with
    its strings plucked in poised delight.

Seeds take route and vegetation grows in the warm soil
    bed
and the animals return with their newborns in a
    conforming lyrical stead.

The brushing flowers in bloom pedal across the florid
    walking way
and the unfolding of the night sky gently appears later
    in the day.

Thawing ice married with the climate so kindly mild
helps the trees to bear seasonal fruit, picked by the
    subtle hands of a smiling child.

For the renewed breeze that courses down the hilly
    slope,
the glistening beauty of spring gifts an aura of
    unwavering hope.

Cycles

The tree stranding tall said to the grass beneath its
    feet,
Thank you for the comfort, for the warm and
    supporting seat.

And the grass said to the birds, gliding in the brisk air,
Thank you for your voices, your singing is gentle and
    fair.

And the birds singing their songs, said to the estuary
    flowing down the mountain crest,
Thank you for the water you give, for the cool splashes
    that chill my heating chest.

And the estuary that passes water to the river body
    said to the rock that stops their speed,
Thank you for providing control; your decorative
    landscape is to the eyes a deed.

And the rocks secured within the stream said to the
    bear that walks on its frame,
Thank you for giving me purpose, for now you can
    cross the stream without any shame.

And the bear that walks over the estuary rocks said to
    the apple gripping the stick,
Thank you for giving me food, a delicious meal that I
    can so easily pick.

And finally, the apple that perches on the stick said to
    the tree,
Thank you for providing me with a home; there's
    nowhere else I'd rather be.

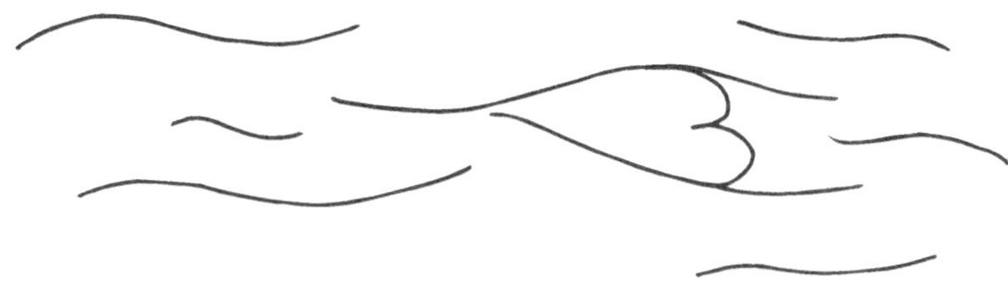

A Wave of Love

A wave of love drifting precariously in the wind,
vacillating in a fierce whirlwind of hopeful chagrin.

Searching for resolution, aiming for longevity,
grasping nothing but the mirage of sly brevity.

For years languishing, longing for its silver lining, a lost
    dove;
cocooned inside a life of ignorance, unaware of what it
    can be: love.

Unable to feel its own charm, its own warmth, its own
    entity,
it is encased by the choking carapace of doubt, blind to
    its true identity.

And then, the sight of another love.

Its lustre marks a euphoric shift, settling splendidly in
    position,
though its presence may be injurious, its harmony
    confounded by unavailing ambition.

Love: a thought so primordial, yet its complexity
    transcends all ages;

its enigmatic aura cannot be contained within a book
    of a thousand pages.

In its primitive permanence, it persists strong and
    unspoiled,
its nebulous string of definition has yet to be uncoiled.

Ensconced within the intricate folds of our very
    existence,
our spirits are drawn to all-encompassing love,
perceived from an insuperable distance.

Goals

About that pitiless place she wanders, a denizen
of the valley of aimless guidance;
through the viscid mud she trudges, yet stays
    imprisoned in that land of subsidence.

Resolved to soldier through the sinking mud,
her feet plough through the knee-deep dirt
for if she stands still she will sink,
and the conscious plateau of life's movement she must
    strive to avert.

A predatory species will hastily die when it forgets the
    compulsion to kill its prey —
and humans who are directionless through life, who
    lose the drive to chase their desires, are doomed to
    walk the same path every day.

How wretched is the horse with blinding blinkers that
    occlude his lateral sight.
For a narrow view to a specific target blackens all
    other lanes, leaving a lonely light.

Presuppositions and narrow goals should be wrestled
    gamely, with shoulders and knees;
only then can the window of life be opened to new
    realities.

Aims are paramount for purposeful living, though they
    must not inhibit digression;
for digression can be a surging stream to an
    electrifying newfound soul's expression.

Seizing on those moments when one's choices in life
    are not compelled
will result in a life of purpose, wherein the value of
    freedom is upheld.

Purpose

The human heart is filled with passion —
blissful, unwavering, excitable passion.

Beauty, love, and kindness: these are what we stay
    alive for,
these earthly gifts of time,
differentiating living from mere existence.

Our lives are imbued with innate purpose;
if ever we tremble under leaden shackles,
we need only to feast our eyes on the summer skies,
on the golden-tinged beams of the daytime sun
and on the velvet night when the stars are strung;
then we will find love within life.

When a shooting star streaks through the blackness,
amid the deafening wails of man's forlorn soul: make
    a wish.

For out of the chaos, there will emerge a beautiful
    calm.
And that dichotomy is what will grant life its purpose.

Time

Time is a miraculous thing. Time loans life its meaning
whilst simultaneously drawing the engagement of
death closer in a ceaseless tyrannical motion.

If birth is the beginning and death is the ostensible
end, time is the comfortable lining between the
two.
And like the lives that it so tightly binds, it is
necessarily finite.

The meagreness of time grants humanity a magnificent
sense of awe and oneness with the world; time's
wonder is augmented by its ephemeral nature.

The mere experience of ageing profoundly contributes
to the understanding of accomplishment. Should
time be indefinitely prolonged, making ageing
obsolete, the preciousness of our engagement with
the world would depart; should time be extended,
the value in the years would subside.

So by extending time, the urgency to capitalise on its
beauty would weaken;
humans' most enjoyable experiences in life are met
with the stark apprehension of urgency.

In the vain pursuit of everlasting time, we are also
dismissing the fact of death.
This failure to accept death will lead us to an
unbearable state of despair when it inexorably
arrives.

It is only by accepting the natural life-cycle that we
will have a more fearless and pleasant death,
and that we will appreciate those few priceless
moments that time affords.

Reason and Passion

The soul is often a perilous battlefield upon which
reason and judgment wage war against passion and
appetite.

The Mediator, if able, would turn the rivalry of the
elements into a mellifluous air.

Your logic and your passion are your armour and your
weapon, undying foes in the arena of your wartime
soul.
If either armour or your weapon be broken, you
will invite strikes without retaliation, or else be
suspended defenceless mid-trench.

For reason ruling alone is a force restrictive and
emotionless; and passion unattended is a predator
with insatiable hunger.

So let your soul direct your passion with reason. And
let your reason be scripted with the flaming pen of
passion.

Neither should be neglected, nor favoured; for he who
is more mindful of one loses the love and the faith
of both.

Among the hills, where the trees grow in purposeful harmony, it is clear that reason rests in the forest.

Yet through the harsh forest fire that blazes through the innocent leaves, it is clear that passion rests in the forest.

Like an arcane forest at the mercy of the elements, you too shall rest in the cool shade of reason and move with passion's fire.

Wilting Leaves

The transience of a wilting springtime leaf is, when
    neglected, rendered doubly brief.

A quotidian watering of the nurtured soil in jolting
    rhythm
promotes the sincere growth of a strong-stemmed
    life's vision.

So easily can we neglect ourselves and others,
smothering life's suffering with thickened covers.

Suffering is a perennial constant that must be
    unambiguously addressed;
the cruellest part of life is the constancy of enduring
    its intensifying quest.

We will forever be akin to springtime leaves, withering
    away when untended;
while confined within the unwholesome soil, our souls
    are unlikely to be mended.

But the arduous climb of consistent internal work
will restore our wilting souls to a proud and vital perk.

For although the labour of growth is painful,

it is the process of growth that makes that growth gainful.

Love's Nuance

The cruel, deep infusion of love with a meaningful
    partner
is a merciful calm succeeding a hungry wind's heavy
    toll
where the piercing swords of absence make cuts that
    leave, in place of a heart, a hole.

There is a battle between delighting in love's
    amusements
enwrapped in the solacing tangle of a shared mind,
and the lament of grating sadness that draws from
    distance
when the search to fill that gaping hole remains so
    unkind.

The Sisyphean boulder pushed up the towering hill
is akin to the thoughtful trembles that frighten the
    lonely heart;
routinely thinking of her, every step, thought, and trill
a doleful departure from that secure, ataraxic start.

Where is she? With whom? And why?
Mournful questions darting around a paper-walled
    mind;

the disillusionment of her absence that we aim to
    justify
manifests the solemn imprint of longing in love,
ever tinged with a yearning unkind.

Belief

As a child, I submitted to the Great Power that rules
the world;
I earnestly prayed that Their kindness would one day
be unfurled.

To my impressionable mind, life's purpose had been
presented by a clean-gowned waiter
but what was served as objectivity was, in fact, belief;
an obstinate faith in an unquestionable Creator.

Faith — like the lustre of a scenic sunset — can either
be seen in its beauty or eclipsed by a journeying
cloud;
it comes from a place of intrinsic humility, and cannot
be conjured up or forcefully endowed.

For years, I have envied those lucky enough to hold the
delight of faith,
those who find fulfilment and identity through God
and their mysterious wraith.

Yet, we need not be fettered by the doctrines
inculcated in youth;
we have the agency to search for meaning and discover
our own inner truth.

Faith is an inherent disposition, a fortunate feature, a
visceral sensation.
Let our minds accept its presence and its absence; to
brighten the diverse paths to internal elation.

Defenceless Joy

Some days I feel like a tall, proud candle on a stable
    metal plate,
and other days I feel the wax melt like tears wetting my
    cheek with anchoring weight.

Some days I am inextinguishable flame burning
    brilliantly with glaring light,
but other days my flame is smothered, and no force can
    repair me to my former might.

The tree that bears fruit can be life-giving and
    plentiful,
yet that same tree can be fruitless when the
    environment is condemnable.

When the grating sounds of misery drown out our
    hopeful voice,
let us swim in that fear and open our ears to that
    wretched noise: a courageous choice.

Some days we may feel that a black smoke suffocates
    us,
as if a morose cocoon enveloping our joy has been
    built;
but this should not be accompanied by shame,

for a head draped in shame never merits the guilt.

Feeling sad is nature's will, as the rising sun
    necessitates a complementary fall.
We must embrace both the highs and the lows; in light,
    strong and in darkness, small.

Finding comfort in the oscillation of life is a formidable
    and strenuous task,
but the quest for this comfort is what will unburden us
    of pride's ruinous mask.

Burning Cloth

Our land is littered with unguarded fuel, and a
   clandestine fire crawls at its feet.
We can smell the fumes, yet cannot see the smoke.
We can feel its ominousness, yet cannot encage it.

Around us, there is inhumanity — people being
   belittled, mistreated, killed.
A history, an identity, a life; tethered to the choking
   chains of oppression.
But there is seldom unrest.

Days pass by, weeks, months, and unless the knife
   is penetrating your own back, it is as if the knife
   weren't there, an invisible blade of oblivion.

But behind the shielding cloak of ignorance lies an
   incessant cycle of mistreatment, pain and carping
   judgement.
No matter where it is – it hunts with a silent vigour.

People are suffocating under the barbaric gaze of
   the oppressor — inhuman, bigoted prying eyes,
   defended by fabricated fear.
Let this fuel us with fervent passion, with unwavering
   ambition, with conscious resolve to act;

never shall we let this ambition be palliated by our
satisfaction, by our comfort.

The knife that cuts five inches deep is no less fatal once
retrieved by three inches, or even once removed.
The gash must be attended to carefully until it heals.

Let us not be a Band-Aid for a bleeding wound, nor
blinded eyes to the burning cloth. We must keep
our conscience at work and our eyes open.

Let us reflect on how we can use our position to better
the lives of those who need it more than ourselves.

Let us remove the knife, care for the wound, and stop
the system that continually feeds on wickedness.

Let us make the change.

Oh, Father

Oh, Father, I am a scared and lonely soul, marooned in
   a dejected angst on life's isolated atoll.

Oh, Father, if only man's heart weren't so unforgiving
that he would let others sink into the doleful depths of
   lifeless living.

The consuming darkness of fear engulfs all humanity;
the ascendancy of light is a child's naive vanity.

Oh, Father, tell me why my lot has been cast
to wish for a future better than the past.

Should I long for happiness, a mirage for the
   wretched?
Or should I yield to my fate, forever tormented?

Oh, Father, when will the blackened souls rest
so that they might, for a moment, cease to be
   oppressed?

I fear that protracted piercing dark night —
Oh, Father, I fear —
that its secret will uncover no hope of delight.

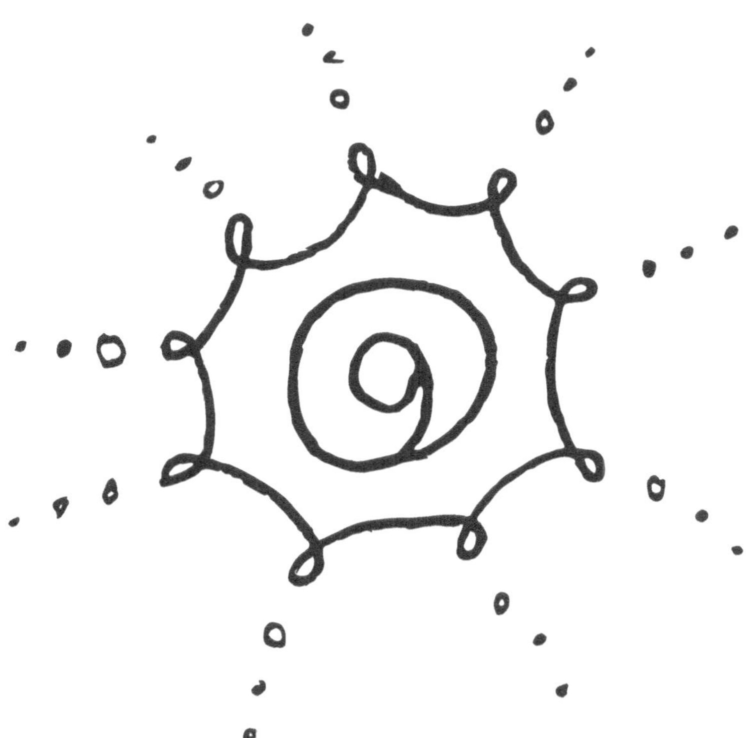

Icarus

A father's gift: a set of well-woven wings,
and a child's merriment at what that endowment
    brings.

The prelude of a sun-kissed, colour-stitched summer's
    sky
belies the peril of an heroic, ill-fated ambition to fly.

Out of the night that eclipses a blinded drive
emerges the folly to depart from a father's guide to
    survive.

"Not too close to the sun or the ocean" is the father's
    decree,
yet heavenward still he soars, in foolish ecstasy.

The destiny of his heedless son is simple to foretell;
the young divinity, his will, his passion and his life,
    bidding to sell.

Icarus' waxen wings melted in the oppressive heat of
    the sun's rays
and the following days met the gods with unrestrained
    dismay.

For the son of a god, so collected and shrewd, had let
   insubordination ferment, so ruination brewed.

From the unforgiving sky Icarus fell, carried down by
   the flooding of gods' tears;
into the sea he plunged, choking on the unruly waters
   of his ambitious years.

His arrogance and imprudent lack of humility
paved the path of his truncated future and
   forthcoming futility.

If only in the words of the wise he had trusted;
then his untimely demise would have been avoided,
and his mind uncorrupted.

Shame

There is a seismic hesitation in facing the unknown
in exiting the orbit of our comfort zone.

Fear leaks from our pores in a trickling drip
as we cling to our shields with tenacious grip.

Yet it is only when we dance with our oppressive fear
that we experience true delight, and life's path
        becomes clear.

Vulnerability is a feeble virtue, according to the
        toughest souls,
but it is vulnerability that empowers us to reach the
        grandest of goals.

Basking in the shadow of our shame and recognising
        our imperfection
allows our humanity to shine onto others — a faithful
        and uncorrupted projection.

The strength to turn up without foreknowledge of
        success
is power beyond winning; it is self-growth and true
        progress.

Reckoning with the inability to control fortune's
    chaotic storm
is the greatest feat of courage that the human spirit
    can perform.

With truth, assertiveness and kindness as the guiding
    principles of our moral creed,
we can overcome shame by embracing the role of
    vulnerability in the life we lead.

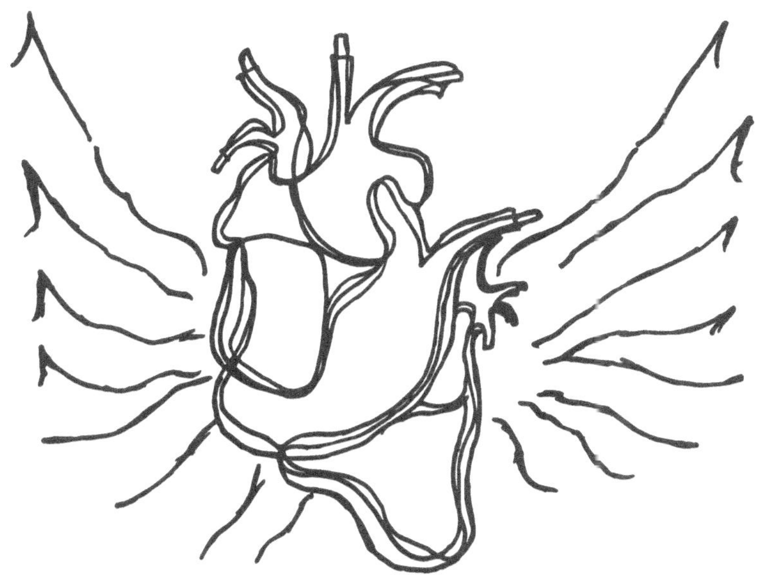

Tenuous Love

The prolonged ache of a breaking relationship is the
    subtle agony of the distance between two.

A source of laughter that was stolen away,
a moment of giving no longer within reach;
a conversation that can never be.
All of the pages of that half-filled story now ripped
    out, burnt and forgotten.

The silence —
the silent cries of glass souls as they shatter so
    stealthily,
reduced once more to mounds of sand.

You cannot bury a broken soul in the stormy winds,
    but merely let it flow,
flying until it is united with the elements.

Still, a single word unspoken amounts to the death of
    an infinite potential, a universe forever erased.

The fear —
fear of emptiness, fear of not being wanted, fear of
    being a stranger to the one who once had your
    heart.

Your heart was pulverised and stomped; as if it were a
    worthless plaything.

But there is a remedy.
The love and care that would be extended by a
    generous heart can be reciprocated by another.
Finding fresh love, finding your perfection, finding a
    part of yourself in someone else:
this does not mend a broken soul.
It creates one anew — an inexhaustible fount of
    rejuvenation.

With this love,
the silence is but a blessing.
With this love,
no shackles or mindful prisons can hold you down,
or let you wallow in the marsh of unease.

It is a pair of wings that, without being worn, could
    never be understood.
These wings not only let you fly;
they let you soar atop the mightiest mountains,
    surveying the expansive and calming view from
    heaven's aspect.

Only then do you realise you have been blinded your
    entire life.
And now, you can see.

Death

A wave of discomfort and sour rage stirs across the
   lashing ocean before, finally, the echoing torrent
   lulls to an ache that manifests as the ebb and flow
   of the ocean shore.

To the dead, the sorrows of living are meaningless.
But to the living: in memory, a flood of grief and
   loneliness.

Death is no merciful human netting.
Death will not comfort or control.
Death will tear away with its demonic talons and will
   eat at the flesh of the innocent.

No remedy will assuage the anguish and desolation of
   those left behind — but that of companionship.

Friendship and comfort are the only little tear of
   succour to the troubled minds and lonely souls.
Without companions, life's wretchedness runs deeper
   and more severe for those who shoulder the
   breaking atrophies of life's absence.

For a room will shine brighter by the burning of many
candles than the burning of a single flame, and
the tenebrous night's twinkle will be most brilliant
when the night is dark.

The living brings itself to its grave from the poison of
longing, whilst the dead torments the living.
However, the dead will perish with death whilst the
living will endure, recover, grow.

Strength sits at the feet of the living and is heaved up
by courage and time and, when used, seizes the
ability to overcome pain.

Human solidarity confers an innate strength that
remains resistant to despotism; its prominent
power can sway the bad into a place of good, the
sick to a place of health, the poor to riches.

Nonetheless, the mystery of death is still that terror
that reduces all to apprehension and dejection.
No person of any social grading can avoid the writhing
vines of fear that ascend from death, as a burning
home cares not for who remains inside.

The many words left unsaid are like the piercing
   knife that penetrates sorrowful minds, prompting
   perpetual pangs of regret; a steadfast force that
   cuts and scars.

How, when one is gone, can those left behind ever
   rationalise the time spent together as satisfactory
   — that the words spoken were ever enough, the
   actions noticed, the smiles consumed?

The vacancy of truth and the forbidden unknown will
   callously prey at the living, vexing the hollowing
   bones of the doubtful.

Death is apprehended by none but Death.

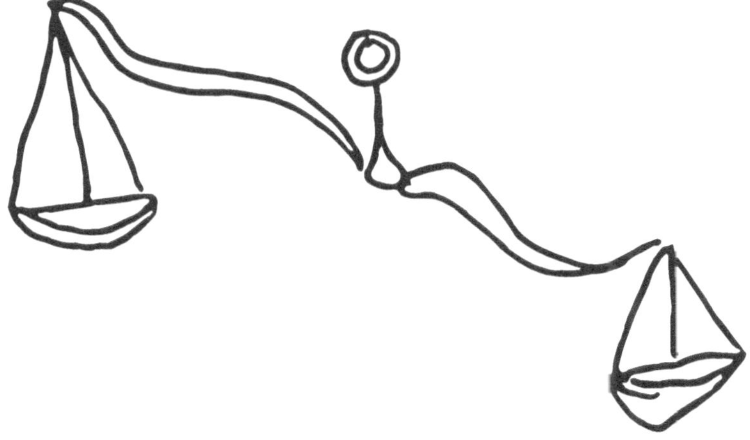

The Broken Scale

An injustice that is met with silent acquiescence;
ignorance, inconsideration, benighted adolescence.

Speaking in a presumptuous, imperious way;
feeding — with bellicose eyes — on vulnerable prey.

Uttering callous words to cause harm, humiliation, and
    guilt
because of who one is, where one is from, and how one
    was built.

Racism, concealed as frail patriotism and stoked by
    fear,
is merely a paucity of heart, a warlike cloud that rains
    bitter tears.

Being kind to others is not an absence of targeted
    bigotry;
it is a basic act of civility, a holy ground for humanity, a
    sacred responsibility.

Performative concealment of prejudice for the benefit
    of social praise
is the bloody glove used to release the caged dove into
    a ruthless blaze.

When we start treating others with tolerance, humility
and understanding,
the world can strike like a piercing arrow to a place of
peace and communal banding.

Let us carefully choose the words we speak, and expel
the vapours of bigotry thereof,
so that we may treat others fairly, and extend the
pleasures of uncompromised love.

Kindness

Pure kindness is not an unreachable, nebulous
abstraction.
It is a gentle smile, a tender hug, an open ear, a
purposeful action.

Kindness is a lone raindrop in the pond where
imprisoning weeds police;
its ripple reverberates through the oppressive grass in
an all-encompassing, flowing crease.

Although it holds a formidable power, a force that
cannot be tamed,
its influence far exceeds the exalted sound of its hallowed
name.

Like a book whose pages are read over and over, yet
whose message persists unspoiled,
no matter how much kindness is shown, its restorative
potential remains ready and coiled.

Let kindness live through its own daily shedding — a
consistent, virtuous resurrection — and, like the
phoenix, rise above its own ashes in a vitalising
projection.

Kindness, like a flame that flickers unperturbed amidst
    a tumultuous, unruly gale,
is undaunted by the turns of fate, like a brave ship with
    uncharted waters to sail.

Today, let us strive to be that spark of kindness that
    lights another's heart,
so that they are ablaze with the fires of compassion,
and imprinted with love's permanent warming mark.

Unknowns

How do you swim in the lake that isn't flowing?
What do you reap when you don't know what you're
    sowing?

Where do you run when you don't know what you're
    racing?
What do you fill when you don't know what you're
    replacing?

How do you see when your eyes are never open?
How do you dream when you continue being woken?

Love, this life is long, and when all the lines are gone
you're on my mind, yet I'm walking blind.
My feet are sunken in the sand
Love, my heart is in your hand.

Words

There is a distinguishable difference between
    censorship and taking care with the words we say;
curtailing oppression in the guise of speech is a
    necessary judiciousness that keeps cruelty at bay.

Speech is a powerful vehicle, the external embodiment
    of our ideals;
it has the strength to inspire and uplift, or to crush
    under its formidable turning wheels.

We are merely the sum of our actions, and our actions
    include our speech;
we cannot believe that we are kind within and then
    manifest hatred with the words we preach.

Our values must be reflected in what we say or else
    they are not our values at all,
as one who rises by means of hot air is doomed to
    falter and inevitably fall.

Staring into the chasm of the self, our gaze is met with
    nothing more
than the quality of our soul — alone in the blankness
    — the ethos at our core.

When we disseminate hate through language, we
humiliate the fabric of our being.
Instead, we must speak with love and compassion, a
power endlessly freeing.

Giving

Giving of your possessions alone, in truth, is giving of
little.
But giving of yourself is the deed of profounder
transmittal.

What are your possessions, but trifling trinkets that do
nought but come and go?
Giving of your heart is a torrent that surges with
irrepressible might, leaving spirits aglow.

The fictitious fear of tomorrow — that impulsive dread
of material loss —
is precisely the fear of need, empty arms perpetually
crossed.

The fear of that ominous cloud that masks the
salubrious blue, coupled with the concurrent dread
of drought,
together form a paradoxical panic — that of certainty
and, at once, of doubt.

Giving of little from the abundance you have for
hidden desires
is providing a bucket from a water-brimmed well to
violent fires.

Those who give all of what they have are those
    acquainted with true giving;
to be a porous basket through whom life drains — this
    is satisfying living.

It is well to give when asked, but unprompted giving is
    a virtue without bounds;
for tending to the needs of the wailing sufferer is all
    the harder when there are no sounds.

And do not all trees in the orchard deserve to be
    watered, to sate their desire to bloom?
So too should we give freely to everyone, for all souls
    should sample from love's sweet perfume.

No feeling is more emancipating than the open-
    handed provision of a valuable gift;
to find joy in the act of giving, in providing an oar to a
    boat adrift.

The time and care we give to others is an electrifying,
    life-giving ray
that nurses the pastures of humanity, every single day.

Leadership

A ship suspended in turbulent seas will always lurch
and fall
if the rudder has been broken in a wind-struck
maritime brawl.

To repair a wound is an uncertain procedure that a
leader must control,
which contrasts with the nominal duty of an
authoritative figure's role.

For the post of one with authority is simply a position;
leading is an action, the strength to tackle an uncertain
mission.

To act with courage and with passion to effect a
positive change
is the duty of a leader, whose impact extends to an
unmitigated range.

Not all authorisers exercise leadership, and not all
leaders are in a space of authority;
but a leader always exerts an influence, whether or not
in a position of seniority.

Planting a seed and overseeing its growth is authority
    performing a duty,
but when a raging gale threatens the safety of the
    stem, leadership takes charge, in all of its beauty.

A successor who inherits a leader's role owns nothing
    but authority, at heart,
yet the ability to harness that power for good is what
    draws authority and leadership apart.

Leadership demands the provocation of boundaries so
    that social norms are stirred;
and only then can true change be made, and can the
    harmony of progress be heard.

Waves

The oscillating moments of life's precious journey
are like the ebb and flow of an ocean.
Artlessly, one rides a transient wave
until the wave's summit caves into the water's surface
and the need to swim ensues.

At the apex of a colossal wave is found the greatest
    view;
at the bottom, a man marvels jealously at those on top.
Of necessity, he swims.

If only it was known to the covetous man
that the men at the top look down, not in vanity or
    hubris
but in unfiltered and indomitable envy.

And that envy is a stain that turns all roses to a deep
    red,
and only once the envy is retired from his soul
will the white roses become white and the yellow roses
    become yellow again.

For the bottom of the wave is the harbinger of the top
and the top remains itself for a moment only fleeting.

The bottom of the wave is not a place of defeat, but a place of beginning.

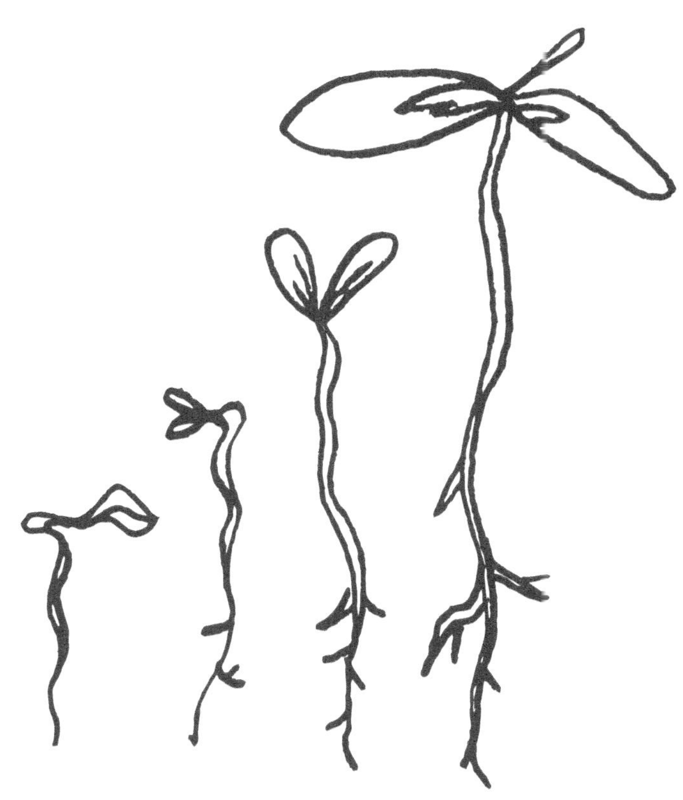

New Life

Entering through the door, warmly cuddled in an
    embracive and gentle hand,
a newborn with charming eyes and shaking paws is
    placed on the floor in a tottered stand.

Tentatively toddling on the flush wooden floor
he slips and skates on frictionless paws
and mops ground with chest from door to door.

His ineffectual tongue strokes new cheeks with
    nervous elation,
as he climbs onto our towering legs with frenzied
    resolve and anticipation.

Disarrayed by a new environment and strangers
    gawping at his youthful leap,
his legs springboard from person to person racing to
    escape the oppressive dusk of sleep.

His pinkish tongue draping out of his mouth whilst his
    paws settle from a zestful shake,
he seizes the bed with a triumphant whimper as his
    ballooning eyes flutter and quake.

A beautiful young friend in the casing of a velvety fur,
akin to a delicate flake in the snow.
Abruptly, he appeared and taught us once again how
to love – welcome home, Marlo.

Family

The closeness of family is the ocean to the parallel sky,
where one is facing the other with a tender and
   protecting eye.

There are spaces between the closeness that allow the
   heavenly winds to dance,
yet the spaces are close enough to bring each member
   to a collective, proud stance.

No matter the distance, time or year,
the unconditional love is memorised in a mellifluous
   melody, distinct and clear.

Supporting each other up close and from afar,
reminding each other that we are beautiful, no matter
   how we feel or where we are.

Confiding in pain and celebrating in delight,
family provides a belt to express vulnerabilities, a
   shining star within a solacing dark night.

An inexpressible love that courses deep from heart to
   mind
that teaches one how to love, be honest and remain
   kind.

The connectedness does not subdue individual merit
    and glow,
as the maple and cypress trees grow in harmony, not in
    each other's shadow.

To grow is not to copy, but to learn and adapt,
as the veins of a tree do not superimpose one another,
    but rather find soil untapped.

So family should not copy to outcompete and duplicate
    what is already there,
but instead support each other in growth, allowing
    new breaths of fresh air.

When there is unquestioned love, and that love burns
    rife,
there can be beauty found in family and beauty found
    in life.

Wonders of a Sunset

A sunset is but the world's most beautiful privilege;
its eminence cannot be expressed through word or
    image.

The flickering retreat of another day, when all is good
    in the world,
it portrays beauty beyond humanity, a domain yet to
    be unfurled.

Despite its temporary visit, a fleeting existence,
the reassurance that it reoccurs inspires wilful
    persistence.

Occasioning a state of felicity unmatched,
its unconquerable presence is beauty manifested, with
    joy attached.

It accentuates every laugh, positive thought or feeling
    of bliss,
fostering a moment of tranquillity for the soulful
    spirits to kiss.

Its arresting grandeur is a force of humility,
a presentation grounding all in a cemented docility.

Its universal grace lavishes serenity upon those in its
wake;
a glimmer of chance and a touch of hope, there for all
to take.

Distant Love

Another sleepless night thinking of you.
I was wishing to the sky and the stars and the moon,
    that our love will never die.

Another sleepless night embracing old photos and
    dancing with the memories.
The magical harmony of the past; something so foreign
    yet so familiar.
Listening to our songs and wearing a calm smile, it was
    another sleepless night.

Waltzing to the highs, and swaying to the lows, a
    tale of hope for the hopeless foes, it was another
    sleepless night.

A sleepless night re-living messages and revising
    lullabies of our love.
Creating new declarations of love and helplessly
    gazing at the clear orange wall that made the subtle
    horizon.

Marvelling at the lustrous sun-kissed sky, a remnant of
    a profound sunset, it was another sleepless night.

Furled in a blanket of fear, and the stitching of the
cosmos stars so near, I called to the darkest of light:
it was another sleepless night.

Candles

With the lighting of a candle dawns the poetic
    potential of humanity
that wields the power to teach kindness.

A candle can donate its flame to a neighbouring wick
whilst retaining its lustrous spark.
A candle, like that of kindness, can give without losing.

The neighbouring candle can now embody a fervent
    flame
whilst the original candle continues its vibrant glow
    unmoved.

Kindness, when utilised, can empower another
    whilst leaving the donor unchanged, if not too
    empowered.

More: a single flame can brighten an entire room.
Even in the deep night, in a room burdened by a heavy
    blanket of darkness,
a candle can illuminate the room and everything
    within it.

And as kindness can burn small, it can echo through
    and fill the once blackened holes,

for kindness can brighten a dark mind and an empty
    soul.

When the heart lies hollow and ghostly,
the presence of kindness can animate it to an ardent
    whole.

Like a candle, to give without losing, and to illuminate
    from the smallest beginning,
kindness is not only life's means, but its compassionate
    end.